Note of Deep Appreciation

To my gifted friends and colleagues, including but not limited to Steven Nisenbaum, Karen Gross, Libby Kiszner, and Tom Pollak, for teaching me so much and supporting me so well for so long...

To my cover and book designer, Asya Blue, and my cover and interior illustrator, Geoffrey Munn, for helping me with their extraordinary talents to bring *What's Your Story* and *Brainy* to life...

To my amazing clients, who have shown me how much better people's lives can become by knowing more about the brain and their relationship with it...

To my beloved granddaughter and special contributor to this book, Gabby Robbins, for her brilliant consultation and blessing of *Brainy* from the start...

To the rest of my kind, smart, beautiful, and funny children and grandchildren, for the joy and light they bring to my life story just by who they are and how they live in the world...

My Heartfelt Thanks!

A Personal Development Workbook for Kids

WHAT'S YOUR STORY?

Building Your Best Adventures In School and Life

Madelaine Claire Weiss
Special Contribution by **Gabby Robbins**

WHAT'S YOUR STORY?
BUILDING YOUR BEST ADVENTURES
IN SCHOOL AND LIFE
By Madelaine Claire Weiss
With Special Contribution by Gabby Robbins

© Copyright 2024 Madelaine Claire Weiss

ISBN 979-8-9908942-1-1 hardcover
ISBN 979-8-9908942-0-4 paperback
ISBN 979-8-9908942-2-8 ebook

Published by

MindOverMatters, LLC
2425 L Street, NW
Washington, DC 20037
www.madelaineweiss.com

Cover and book design by Asya Blue Design
Cover and interior Illustrations by Geoffrey Munn

Contents

Welcome!

Brainy is not a real brain, of course. Brainy is a cartoon character created to teach kids about conversations they have with their brains. Have you ever noticed your conversations with your brain? We call it thinking.

Thinking is like a private conversation we all have with our brains about what is happening in the world, what we hope will happen, what the challenges may be, and how we will try to make our lives as amazing as we can. Sometimes thinking makes things better. Sometimes thinking makes things hard.

The more we know about the brain, the more we can work together with it to fill our lives with great adventures that are more interesting and fun—in school and life.

We are going to focus on stories, how the brain makes up stories for us to live in, and how knowing this can help us build even better life stories for ourselves. And when we talk about what makes a great story, you will get to write stories of your own.

I hope you will be as excited about our journey as I am and I wish you all the best adventures in school and life.

With Love,
Madelaine

Hi, My Name is Brainy and I Will Be Your Guide.

What's Your Name?
You Can Write It in the Box.

Great, Thank You! Let's Get Started...

PART 1

Once Upon a Time

CHAPTER 1

How Stories Got Started

First, I want to tell you how your brain uses stories to make your life better. Then we'll talk about how you and your brain can work together to create your own amazing life stories.

Are you ready? Let's try this now.

Look at this picture. What story do you see?

Hint: Many stories are possible.

Your story could be about...

- Planting another tree to keep the first tree company.

- Digging a hole for your dog to bury their bone.

- Putting in a sign that says: Please Do Not Litter.

- OR maybe it's about releasing your frustration by seeing how deep you can dig.

You can write your own story about what is happening in the picture. Remember, there are no right or wrong answers. All answers can be great! You can use a separate piece of paper if you like.

Here it is again. Now, let's start having fun creating stories on the next page!

Your Story About What is Happening with The Kids Digging a Hole

_____

_____

_____

_____

_____

_____

_____

_____

_____

_____

_____

_____

If your friend looked at the same picture, they might write a different story about it. So, let's look at an old story that will show how different brains can think different things!

Imagine six blindfolded friends, each trying to describe an elephant. One brave soul, touching the trunk, thought it felt like a slippery snake. Another, feeling the elephant's side, said it was solid like a wall. The one holding the tusk said it was like a spear. The one touching the knee said it was like a tree.

The one touching the ear said it was like a fan. And another, holding the tail, said, "Oh no, you are all wrong. It is like a rope." Oh my, did they argue! "No, you are wrong!" they shouted at each other.

And guess what? They were all right, in a way. But none of them were completely right because none of them felt the whole elephant.

This teaches us that our thoughts are not facts. They are more like stories we tell ourselves. And it's all thanks to our amazing brains!

Speaking of brains, let's see one! Ta-da! It looks something like this.

We'll explore how it works and what it does soon. Right now, I want you to know that brains have been storytellers for ages.

Way back, about 40,000 years ago, people's brains helped them draw pictures on cave walls (yes, they lived in caves!). Even before that, 120,000-700,000 years ago, brains helped folks tell stories around the campfire.

These stories taught them how to be kind and handle problems like scary animals and bad weather.

Nowadays, stories are in books and on screens, and they're super fun.

But there's so much information out there! Imagine the whole universe having six times 70 million zeros bits of information. It's mind-boggling!

And guess what else? Your eyes, nose, ears, mouth, and skin send a whopping 11,000,000 bits of information to your brain every second. But here's the kicker—your brain can only handle about 50 bits of all that.

So, what do brains do? Brains try their best to turn that tiny bit of information into a story that makes sense. But sometimes even brains make mistakes.

Sometimes it can look like a snake when it's only a rope. So, sometimes your brain might tell you something's not safe when actually it is. Or it might say an idea isn't good, even if it could be fantastic!

But hold on. What if you and your brain teamed up? Like Superheroes, the more you work together, the more amazing your adventures in school and life will become!

I like to call brains story-making machines, even though a brain is not really a machine. In the next chapter, I am going to tell you all about that!

CHAPTER 2

The Story-Making Machine

Let's take a closer look at your incredible brain. It's not really like a twirling, clanking machine with gears and levers. But you can think of it as a magical story-making machine that spins ideas and stories for you every day.

Your brain is like a super-smart computer. It can remember things, just like when you save photos or files on a computer.

Your brain can do lots of things at the same time, like walking, talking, and thinking all at once.

Just like you click and type on a computer so it knows what to do, your brain talks to your body. And your body talks to your brain. This is how they figure out what's happening and what to do next.

The way messages go back and forth makes your brain a bit like a super-smart computer—but it's not really a computer.

Now, your brain isn't a garden either, but it's a little bit like one. People plant tiny seeds in a garden that can grow into beautiful flowers or yummy veggies.

Learning something new is like planting tiny seeds in your brain that can grow into wonderful things you know and can do.

Sometimes, people need to pull out weeds in a garden to help the good plants grow. Gardens also need water and sunshine to grow.

Your brain needs new experiences, practice, and healthy habits to help you grow.

You can also think of your brain as a super special car.

Learning something new, like math, a sport, or a musical instrument, is like turning the key for your brain's engine. Your brain then takes you on a journey to get good at that new thing.

Just like a car needs fuel and maintenance, your brain needs good food, exercise, and rest to keep running. And just like a car can go in different directions, your brain can think of different ways to solve problems and make cool things happen.

It's like your brain is driving you on adventures—even though a brain is not really a car.

Brains are involved in everything you think, feel, and do. They are super complicated. Scientists don't understand everything about brains yet, but here's some of what they do know that can help us.

Your brain is a 3-pound blob of super-smart jelly. I'm just kidding. Even though it is squishy like jelly and has a lot of water and sugar in it, your brain is not made of jelly.

Your brain has billions of cells called neurons. Neurons look like little octopuses. Everything we feel, think, and do happens when neurons send tiny sparks of messages to each other.

Your brain also has different parts, like pieces of a puzzle.

There are upper and lower parts. The upper part helps you learn new things and make decisions. The lower part takes care of things you don't even have to think about, like your heartbeat and breathing.

There is also a right side and a left side, called hemispheres. We use both sides.

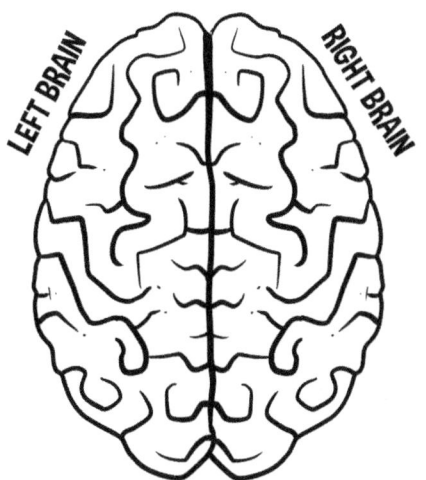

Researchers have said that the right side is amazing at creativity and imagination. It helps you dream up stories or draw pictures. The left side is great at thinking logically. It helps you to solve problems and understand words and numbers.

These parts must work together like a team to help you with everything you do. The better they work together, the better you can make decisions about your life story.

Before we move on, you may be wondering, "What is the Mind?" Is it the same or different from the brain?

That's a tricky one, and scientists are still trying to figure it out. But it has something to do with awareness and paying attention to what's going on inside and outside of you. The mind includes your past experiences too.

The mind isn't physical stuff like the brain. It's more like a story that's always being written in your head.

In Part 2, Happily Ever After, I'll show you a quick and easy brain fitness tool.

Exercise makes your body strong. This brain fitness tool will help your brain be strong so you can create great stories and adventures for yourself in school and life.

But what makes a great story? Let's find out!

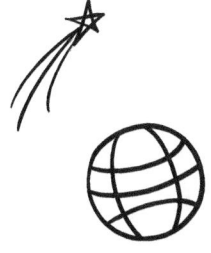

CHAPTER 3

What Makes a Great Story

Many times, your brain goes off on its own, making up stories for you to live in. The word for this is unconscious. It means that you don't even know why you are thinking, feeling, and doing as you do.

Sure, you can't do anything without your brain. You need your brain to be a great partner, but not to be in charge, especially if you don't even know what it's doing.

The idea is for you to give your brain more and better directions so you are more in charge.

In the next section, you will write stories about your life. You will need to know what kind of directions to give your brain to make your stories great.

There are lots of different ways to tell a great story. It's like picking different colors to paint a picture or choosing pieces to build a Lego castle. We're going to use something I like to call *The Story Map* to help guide you through your story.

This map is a simpler version of what Joseph Campbell called the Hero's Journey. Campbell noticed that many great stories worldwide followed a similar pattern, like steps in a dance.

The Story Map uses the steps of the journey to help you create your own amazing stories.

Like a hero in a story, you will face challenges and opportunities in life. By working with your brain and other people, you can become stronger and happier.

Here is The Story Map:

What's Happening

The hero is facing a challenging situation.

What's Possible

The hero discovers a resource or ally to assist.

What's Next

The hero takes action to deal with the challenge.

Happily Ever After

The hero succeeds, leading to a positive outcome.

Would you like an example? Let's do Harry Potter.

1. What's Happening: Harry Potter is living with mean relatives. He finds out he's a wizard! He goes to a magical school called Hogwarts and meets new friends.

2. What's Possible: Harry is helped by friends, cool magic lessons, and kind teachers. He also learns to be really brave, just like his parents.

3. What's Next: Harry discovers a secret about a magical stone. He faces sneaky challenges and comes face-to-face with a bad wizard!

4. Happily Ever After: Harry and his friends save the day! He finds a place where he belongs. Harry feels happy and ready for more magical adventures.

Okay, one more, Matilda.

1. What's Happening: Matilda is super smart but has mean parents. She goes to school and discovers she can move things with her mind!

2. What's Possible: Matilda's secret powers and very nice teacher help her deal with school bullies and her mean parents.

3. What's Next: Matilda cleverly uses her special powers to fix unfair things at home and school. She also helps Miss Honey with a big problem.

4. Happily Ever After: Things get better for Matilda and Miss Honey. Matilda finds a happy home with Miss Honey. She feels loved and understood.

Then, the four parts of The Story Map can be combined into a paragraph to make it read like a real story, like this:

Matilda is super smart but has mean parents. She goes to school and discovers she can move things with her mind! Her secret powers and very nice teacher, Miss Honey, help her deal with school bullies and mean parents. Matilda uses her special powers to fix unfair things at home and school. She also helps Miss Honey with her big problem. Things get better for Matilda and Miss Honey. Matilda finds a happy home with Miss Honey. She feels loved and understood.

Your stories can be longer than this one about Matilda. Maybe even 200 words, or more, if you like.

Are we ready for your stories? Just about! First, I have to tell you about a very important topic—The Magic of Happiness!

PART 2

Happily Ever After

CHAPTER 4

The Magic of Happiness

Happiness is something that we have to talk about before we start your stories.

Tough stuff happens sometimes. That's just part of life. So *Happily Ever After* doesn't mean that you're always super excited about everyone and everything that happens.

Happily Ever After means enjoying your everyday adventures in school and life. It is a general feeling that life is good. Whatever Isn't all that good is nothing you can't handle—teamed up with your brain and with the help of other people in your life.

All people have a right to want to be happy. The Declaration of Independence even said that all people had a right to "Life, Liberty, and the Pursuit of Happiness."

A lot of people think it's not okay to want to be happy. They think it's selfish.

But that's not right! Wanting to be happy is not selfish at all! It is wonderful and here is why.

When people are happy they feel good inside and want to spread sunshine to others.

They are more creative. They come up with fun and interesting ideas and adventures. They are also more productive, which means they can get a lot of good things done.

And here's the cool part—happy people are also caring. They like to help others and be kind because they want everyone to feel happy too.

So, when you figure out how to make yourself happier, you're not just improving your own life story. Happy people make the world a brighter and happier place!

Then why isn't everyone as happy as they can be? As we said, hard things happen, and there is not always something you can do about them. But there is something else going on that you can do something about, and it has to do with your brain's memory.

Your brain has a good memory—sometimes too good. Memories are like files. The brain stores them in special folders, which contain information about things you've seen, heard, or felt.

Some memories are good and make you happy, like a fun birthday party. Others can be not-so-good and make you feel upset or scared. *Triggers* are things that happen in the present that remind the brain of a not-so-good memory from the past.

For example, if you got really scared during a lightning and thunderstorm, the next time it started to rain, those feelings could begin to get triggered again. When the brain sees a trigger, it's like an emotional alarm going off. This can make the emotional parts of the brain become super active, like when you feel very scared or angry.

It's important to understand the difference between reacting and responding. You might react quickly without thinking when your emotional parts are super active.

REACT vs RESPOND?

If you touch a hot stove without realizing it's hot, reacting quickly is a good thing. But there are other times when it would be better to think first, which would be responding.

As we said, your brain has different parts. Some parts help you to be creative and solve problems. Other parts take care of things like your heartbeat.

Strong emotions come from a special part of your brain that can make you feel really happy or really upset. Sometimes this part can cause you to react quickly to things before you have time to think.

That's why the brain's parts have to work together as a team. Together they can help you make the kinds of decisions that will make your life great. And there is a way, called *The ATM Way to Happiness*.

No, it's not about money like the ATM people use when they need cash. This way to happiness is not about money at all!

The ATM Way to Happiness will help you and your brain work together. This will help you keep worries from the past and worries about the future from getting in the way. Let's see how it works.

The ATM Way To Happiness

A Acknowledge Your Emotions

If something upsets you, for example, the first thing to do is notice what you are feeling in your body. Your chest might feel heavy. Your stomach or head could even start to hurt.

Acknowledging your feelings first in your body helps keep them from getting too strong. Emotions are important because they tell you that something is going on so you can think about what to do. But when emotions are too strong, even if they are about something good, it can be hard to keep all of the parts together to figure things out.

T Team Up with Your Brain

We talked about the upper part of the brain helping you learn new things and make decisions, and the left side being good at problem-solving. How can you bring these parts back to the team when the emotional parts have gotten in their way? It's simple. Use your breath to build your team!

Here is the instruction. It takes only 30 seconds to get all the important parts working together again. Practice it a lot, and it will become easy for you. I like to call it *Power Breathing*, and you can too.

Stand or sit still and close your eyes gently. Or you may just look down.

Breathe slowly in through your nose, filling up your belly with air like it's a balloon.

Breathe slowly out through your nose, letting the air out of your belly like a balloon.

Do this in and out about three times, making sure the breaths are slow and deep.

Then gently open your eyes and come back into the room.

M Make a Plan

Now that the parts of your brain are working as a team, you can talk to your brain, which you do anyway. It's called thinking. But now you can do it better to help you figure out what you want to do. Or not do.

Sometimes the best action is no action, but you need a good team to figure that out too, using *The Story Map* as your guide. Here they are together, *The ATM Way* and *The Story Map*.

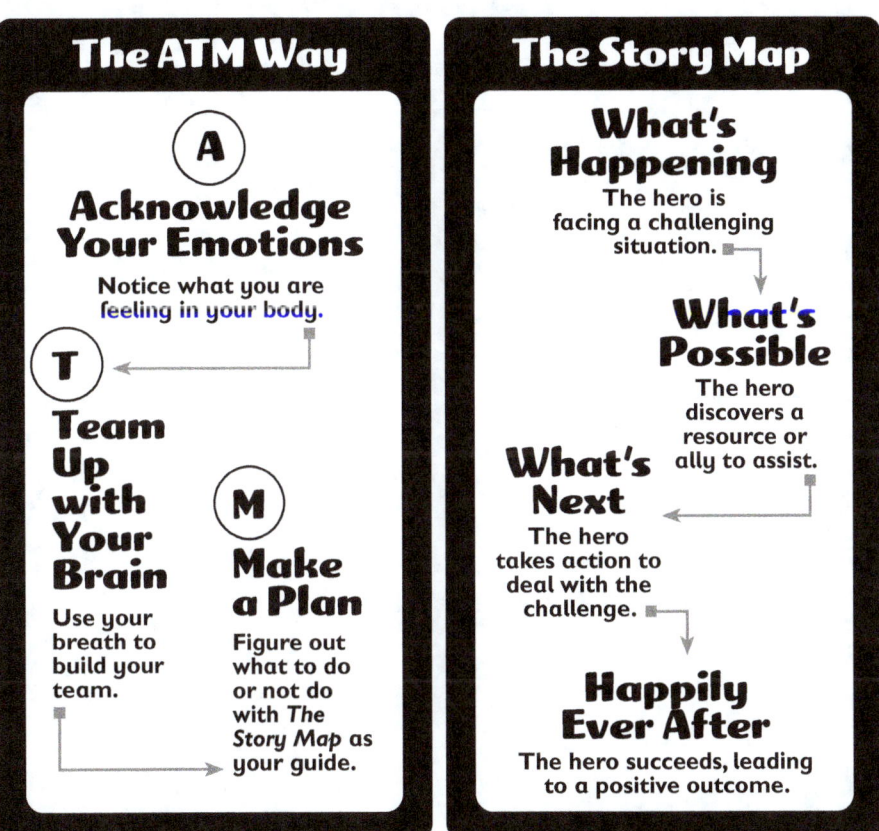

Okay, so now that you know how to make a great team with your brain to make a great story, we are ready for your stories!!

Let's Go!

CHAPTER 5

Inside Relationship Stories

Getting along with yourself and with others are super skills that you need to have a great life. And you need both!

In this chapter, we will start with Inside Relationship Stories and save the Outside Relationship Stories for the next.

For all of the stories, you will fill out *The Story Map* and then you can turn that into a short story you will write.

You may use a separate piece of paper if you like and even draw a picture of your story just for fun.

If you are having trouble or are just curious, you may also go to the *Story Appendix*, starting on page 77, for examples!!

I will give you situations that happen often with kids your age in school and life.

You can build them into great life stories and adventures.

At the end of this chapter, I will also give you a blank worksheet so you can make up a challenge of your own.

For each story you choose, you will practice using *The ATM Way to Happiness* with *The Story Map* as your guide.

Inside Relationship
Story Exercises

Super Tricky Homework

What's Happening

Imagine that you get a homework assignment with words in it that you have never seen before. You are filled with *negative self-talk*. Your brain tells you that you will never be able to figure this out and get it done. It feels to you like the whole rest of your day is ruined.

The ATM Way: *Acknowledge Your Emotions. Then Team Up with Your Brain (Breathe) To Make a Plan for Building Your Best Adventure with The Story Map as Your Guide.*

What's Possible

_____

_____

_____

_____

_____

_____

_____

What's Next

_____

_____

_____

_____

Happily Ever After

_____

_____

_____

_____

_____

_____

_____

_____

_____

Writing Out the Super Tricky Homework Story

Skateboard Struggles

What's Happening

Imagine that you decided to try a new sport and picked skateboarding. You've been practicing in the playground near your house and have been falling all day. You've already skinned your knees and elbows. But that's not the worst part. The worst part is that the other kids are making fun of you, and now you wish you never tried at all.

The ATM Way: *Acknowledge Your Emotions. Then Team Up with Your Brain (Breathe) To Make a Plan for Building Your Best Adventure with The Story Map as Your Guide.*

What's Possible

_____

_____

_____

_____

_____

_____

_____

What's Next

_____

_____

_____

_____

Happily Ever After

_____

_____

_____

_____

_____

_____

_____

_____

_____

Writing Out the Skateboard Struggles Story

_____

_____

_____

_____

_____

_____

_____

_____

_____

_____

_____

_____

_____

Emotional Roller Coaster

What's Happening

Imagine that you didn't sleep well last night. It's been happening more than it should lately, and you don't know why. What you do know is that your emotions feel all over the place inside. Some things are making you happy, others making you mad or scared. It all feels like too much, making everything you have to do at school and home feel too hard.

The ATM Way: Acknowledge Your Emotions. Then Team Up with Your Brain (Breathe) To Make a Plan for Building Your Best Adventure with The Story Map as Your Guide.

What's Possible

_____

_____

_____

_____

_____

_____

What's Next

_____

_____

_____

_____

Happily Ever After

_____

_____

_____

_____

_____

_____

_____

_____

Writing Out the Emotional Roller Coaster Story

_____

_____

_____

_____

_____

_____

_____

_____

_____

_____

_____

_____

_____

Build Your Own Inside Relationship Story

What's Happening

_____

_____

_____

The ATM Way: _Acknowledge Your Emotions. Then Team Up with Your Brain (Breathe) To Make a Plan for Building Your Best Adventure with The Story Map as Your Guide._

What's Possible

_____

_____

_____

_____

_____

What's Next

_____

_____

_____

_____

Happily Ever After

_____

_____

_____

_____

_____

_____

_____

_____

_____

Writing Out Your Own Inside Relationship Story

_____

_____

_____

_____

_____

_____

_____

_____

_____

_____

_____

_____

CHAPTER 6

Outside Relationship Stories

There is more to life than food, water, a place to live, and new sneakers. That was a joke.

Sure, it's important to have your basic needs met. And you and your whole brain getting along is mighty important too. But even all of that is not enough.

People need other people. Just as all the parts of the brain have to get along, people have to get along with each other, or at least try.

From the beginning of history, people have needed each other. They found life easier when they stuck together with their families and friends.

As we said already, they shared food, kept each other safe, and told stories around the campfire.

And guess what? Scientists discovered that we tend to be happier when we have good friends and family. We might even live longer and healthier lives.

Imagine having someone to share your laughs and troubles with. Imagine having someone to help when things are tough, and to cheer for you when you do awesome stuff.

That's how having special people in your life feels—like a big warm hug that helps you feel happy and stay strong.

But it's not always super easy to make friends and get along with everyone. Sometimes, we might feel shy and not sure what to say.

Other people are not always having a good day. When they are not, they are not always that nice. And some people, sometimes right in a kid's own home can have problems that just get in the way.

It's okay. Remember *Happily Ever After* doesn't mean everything is perfect all the time. It's a feeling that life is pretty good. It's a belief that whatever isn't that good is nothing you can't handle either by yourself or with the help of someone who cares.

Outside Relationship Stories will help you think about how to make friends, handle tricky situations, and have even more fun with the people in your life. Let's go there now.

Outside Relationship Story Exercises

Party Problems

What's Happening

Imagine that two school friends invited you to their birthday parties. You would love to go to both, but they are at the same time. You are afraid the friend whose party you don't go to will feel hurt and mad at you. You are frustrated because getting invited to two parties is a good thing that is not supposed to make you feel bad.

The ATM Way: Acknowledge Your Emotions. Then Team Up with Your Brain (Breathe) To Make a Plan for Building Your Best Adventure with The Story Map as Your Guide.

What's Possible

What's Next

_____

_____

_____

_____

Happily Ever After

_____

_____

_____

_____

_____

_____

_____

_____

Writing Out the Party Problems Story

_____

_____

_____

_____

_____

_____

_____

_____

_____

_____

_____

_____

_____

_____

New School Starter

What's Happening

Imagine that your family moved you to a new school where you don't know anyone. You miss your old friends and worry about whether you will ever make any new friends. It feels like it would just be easier not to. But you know it is not good for you to have no friends. It's not fun either, so you feel stuck about what to do or not do from here.

The ATM Way: Acknowledge Your Emotions. Then Team Up with Your Brain (Breathe) To Make a Plan for Building Your Best Adventure with The Story Map as Your Guide.

What's Possible

_____

_____

_____

_____

_____

_____

What's Next

_____

_____

_____

_____

Happily Ever After

_____

_____

_____

_____

_____

_____

_____

_____

_____

Writing Out the New School Starter Story

Messed-Up Room

What's Happening

Imagine that your mom sat you down to discuss your messy room. You think that as long as you close the door, why should anyone else care if there is a big mess in there? Your mom tries to explain that this responsibility is part of growing up. You don't agree. Your mom and you are both upset. And you don't know what to do.

The ATM Way: Acknowledge Your Emotions. Then Team Up with Your Brain (Breathe) To Make a Plan for Building Your Best Adventure with The Story Map as Your Guide.

What's Possible

_____

_____

_____

_____

_____

_____

What's Next

_____

_____

_____

_____

Happily Ever After

_____

_____

_____

_____

_____

_____

_____

_____

Writing Out the Messed-Up Room Story

Build Your Own Outside Relationship Story

What's Happening

_____
_____

_____

The ATM Way: Acknowledge Your Emotions. Then Team Up with Your Brain (Breathe) To Make a Plan for Building Your Best Adventure with The Story Map as Your Guide.

What's Possible

_____

_____

_____

_____

_____

_____

What's Next

_____

_____

_____

_____

Happily Ever After

_____

_____

_____

_____

_____

_____

_____

_____

Writing Out Your Own Outside Relationship Story

Wrap Up
for Now

I hope you enjoyed our time together. I know I did because it means the world to me to share all of this with you through *Brainy*. We love *Brainy* and hope you do too.

A lot of adults tell me they wish someone had told them everything *Brainy* and I just shared with you when they were your age. They wish they knew about how the brain creates stories. They wish they knew how much better their lives could be by working together with their brains as a team, and with other people too.

They believe that if they knew then what you know now their lives could have been so much easier and better.

You can use *The ATM Way to Happiness* with *The Story Map* as your guide any time you want to work on something for the rest of your life. *Power Breathing* is so simple that you can use it anywhere, for any reason. You can use it anytime you want to think, feel, and do better in your life—every day if you feel like it!

The story-making exercises are a way to practice your writing skills. But they are also a way to plant seeds in your brain that can grow into amazing new skills that can last your whole life.

So, to wrap up for now, I want to leave you with something that I believe is true.

This is T.H.E. Truth

T   The truth is that life is a story we make up with our brains. Knowing this can help us to make our life stories even better.

H   Happiness depends on healthy Inside and Outside Relationships. The happier we are the more we can help the world.

E   Emotions provide important information that we need to build our greatest adventures in school and life. They work best alongside all the other parts of our brains teamed up together.

**"The End" is how a lot of books finish.
But with everything you know now,
this is not the end at all.**

This is The Beginning

 Today is the first day of
the rest of your life.

Now you know how to fill it
with even more and better
stories and adventures.

Enjoy!!
Madelaine

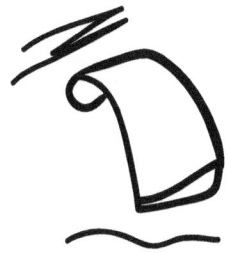

STORY APPENDIX

Examples

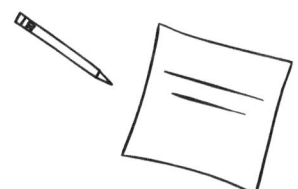

BUILDING YOUR BEST ADVENTURES IN SCHOOL AND LIFE

EXAMPLES

Using The *ATM Way to Happiness*

with

The Story Map as Your Guide

Super Tricky Homework Example

What's Happening

Imagine that you get a homework assignment with words in it that you have never seen before. You are filled with *negative self-talk*. Your brain tells you that you will never be able to figure this out and get it done. It feels to you like the whole rest of your day is ruined.

The ATM Way: Acknowledge Your Emotions. Then Team Up with Your Brain (Breathe) To Make a Plan for Building Your Best Adventure with The Story Map as Your Guide.

What's Possible

I thought about asking my teacher or a classmate for help. I could also use fun websites or books to learn new words. Or maybe I could break the homework into smaller, easier tasks.

What's Next

I decided to be brave and asked my teacher for help. I also used a fun website with games to learn those tricky words and divided my homework into small chunks.

Happily Ever After

With some help and hard work, I finished my homework, and guess what? I understood everything! I felt super proud, and the rest of my day turned out to be awesome!

Example of Writing Out a Super Tricky Homework Story

One day, I got a homework assignment with words I had never seen before. My brain was talking negatively to me, telling me that I was never going to be able to figure this out and get it done.

I felt like the rest of my day would be ruined.

Using *The ATM Way*, I stopped to notice what I was feeling in my body. Then I did my breaths to get my inside team up and ready to figure out how to deal with this using *The Story Map* as my guide.

I thought about asking my teacher or a classmate for help. I could also use fun websites or books to learn new words. Or maybe I could break the homework into smaller, easier tasks.

But I felt funny about letting anyone know I was having trouble.

Finally, I decided to be brave and asked my teacher for help. I also used a fun website with games to learn those tricky words and divided my homework into small chunks.

With some help and hard work, I finished my homework, and guess what? I understood everything!

I felt super proud, and the rest of my day turned out to be awesome!

Skateboard Struggles Example

What's Happening

Imagine you decided to try a new sport and picked skateboarding. You've been practicing in the playground near your house and have been falling all day. You've already skinned your knees and elbows. But that's not the worst part. The worst part is that the other kids are making fun of you, and now you wish you never tried at all.

The ATM Way: Acknowledge Your Emotions. Then Team Up with Your Brain (Breathe) To Make a Plan for Building Your Best Adventure with The Story Map as Your Guide.

What's Possible

I talked to my dad. We both thought asking the older, really good skateboarders for tips could be a good idea. I could also wear protective gear to avoid getting hurt and remind myself how much I wanted to try skateboarding in the first place.

What's Next

I decided to approach an older skateboarder at the park for advice and put on my helmet and pads. Despite the teasing, I kept trying.

Happily Ever After

I kept at it and started doing better. Those same kids who made fun of me began to cheer me on as I landed my first trick. I felt proud of myself for not giving up, and skateboarding became even more fun!

Example of Writing Out a Skateboard Struggles Story

I had been thinking for a while that I would love to try Skateboarding. I practiced at the playground near my house every day and kept falling.

My knees and elbows were bruised, but that wasn't even the worst part.

The worst part was that the other kids were making fun of me. I started to wish that I had never tried, but I didn't want to give up either.

Using *The ATM Way*, I stopped to notice what I was feeling in my body. Then I did my breaths to get my inside team up and ready to figure out how to deal with this using *The Story Map* as my guide.

I talked to my dad. We both thought it would be a good idea to ask the older, really good skateboarders for tips.

I could also wear protective gear to avoid getting hurt and remind myself how much I wanted to try skateboarding in the first place.

And that's exactly what I did. I got advice from an older skateboarder at the park, and put on my helmet and pads. Despite the teasing, I kept trying and actually started to get good at it.

Those same kids who made fun of me were cheering me on as I landed my first trick. I felt proud of myself for not giving up.

Now I skateboard with the best of them and it's really fun!

Emotional Roller Coaster Example

What's Happening

Imagine that you didn't sleep well last night. It's been happening more than it should lately, and you don't know why. What you do know is that your emotions feel all over the place inside. Some things are making you happy, others making you mad or scared. It all feels like too much, making everything you have to do at school and home feel too hard.

The ATM Way: *Acknowledge Your Emotions. Then Team Up with Your Brain (Breathe) To Make a Plan for Building Your Best Adventure with The Story Map as Your Guide.*

What's Possible

I thought about talking to my parents or a trusted adult. Maybe keeping a bedtime routine and finding calming activities like reading or drawing would help with my emotions.

What's Next

I decided to talk to my parents about how I've been feeling and they suggested we create a bedtime routine together. I also started reading a book before bed to help me relax.

Happily Ever After

It took some time, but my sleep improved, and my emotions felt better too. With better rest and support from my family, school and home tasks became easier to handle. I felt happier more of the time.

Example of Writing Out an Emotional Roller Coaster Story

I was having trouble sleeping, tossing and turning all night. It was happening a lot.

It made me worry because I didn't know why it was happening and because it was making my emotions all over the place.

What's up with my brain, and why isn't it helping me to rest when I need to like it is supposed to? One minute, I'm happy, and then I'm sad or mad.

Everything I have to do, or even want to do, at school and home just feels too hard.

Using *The ATM Way*, I stopped to notice what I was feeling in my body. Then I did my breaths to get my inside team up and ready to figure out how to deal with this using *The Story Map* as my guide.

I figured I could talk to someone I trusted to help me get to sleep at the right time every night. I could also do calming activities like drawing or reading to help with my emotions.

So, I did talk to my parents about how I've been feeling and they suggested we create a bedtime routine together.

I also started reading a book before bed to help me relax.

It took some time, but my sleep improved, and my emotions felt much easier.

With better rest and support from my family, school and home tasks got much easier and more fun.

I felt relieved, calmer, and happier most of the time.

Party Problems Example

What's Happening

Imagine that two school friends invited you to their birthday parties. You would love to go to both, but they are at the same time. You are afraid that the friend whose party you don't go to will feel hurt and mad at you. You are frustrated because getting invited to two parties is a good thing that is not supposed to make you feel bad.

The ATM Way: *Acknowledge Your Emotions. Then Team Up with Your Brain (Breathe) To Make a Plan for Building Your Best Adventure with The Story Map as Your Guide.*

What's Possible

I thought about talking to my friends and explaining the situation, suggesting an alternative day to celebrate with the friend whose party I didn't attend, or finding a way to make it up to them.

What's Next

I decided to have an honest conversation with both friends and explained my problem. They understood, and we planned a special day to hang out with the friend whose party I would miss. We also decided I would miss the party that had more kids coming anyway.

Happily Ever After

It turned out better than I thought! My friends appreciated my honesty, and we had a blast on our special day together. I learned that good friends understand and that I don't have to feel sad or worried about having too many invitations

Example of Writing Out a Party Problems Story

I was so excited that I got invited to two parties. Then I realized I could only go to one because they were both at the same time.

I felt afraid that the friend whose party I didn't go to would feel hurt and be mad at me.

And I was mad myself. Isn't getting invited to two parties supposed to be a good thing? Why should I have to feel so bad? And how am I ever going to figure out what to do?

Using *The ATM Way*, I stopped to notice what I was feeling in my body. Then I did my breaths to get my inside team up and ready to figure out how to deal with this using *The Story Map* as my guide.

I thought about talking to my friends, but together or one at a time, or just one, but then which one?

My inside brain team and I decided to have an honest conversation with both friends to explain my problem.

They understood. Together we planned a special day to hang out with the friend whose party I missed.

We also decided I would miss the party that had more kids coming anyway.

It turned out better than I thought! My friends appreciated my honesty, and we had a blast on our special day together.

I learned that good friends understand and that I can be happy instead of worried when I get invited to parties.

New School Starter Example

What's Happening

Imagine that your family moved you to a new school where you don't know anyone. You really miss your old friends and are worried about whether you will ever make any new friends. It feels like it would just be easier not to. But you know it is not good for you to have no friends. It is not fun either, so you feel stuck about what to do or not do from here.

The ATM Way: *Acknowledge Your Emotions. Then Team Up with Your Brain (Breathe) To Make a Plan for Building Your Best Adventure with The Story Map as Your Guide.*

What's Possible

I thought about joining clubs or activities to meet new people. I could also try starting conversations with classmates and give the new school a chance to see if it grows on me.

What's Next

I decided to attend a club that interested me and started saying "hi" to classmates. It was hard at first, but I wanted to give it a shot.

Happily Ever After

Over time, I made new friends who made the new school feel more like home. I realized that change can be tough, but it can also lead to exciting experiences and new friendships

Example of Writing Out a New School Starter Story

It wasn't my idea for my family to move and I wasn't happy about it either.

There I was at a new school where I didn't know anybody. It didn't look like I was going to be making any friends here.

I was feeling really sad, maybe a little mad too, and just wanted my old friends back! I didn't even feel like I wanted to make new friends. It felt like too much trouble.

But I knew that having no friends was not going to be good for me so I had to figure something out.

Using *The ATM Way*, I stopped to notice what I was feeling in my body, then did my breaths to get my inside team up and ready to figure out how to deal with this using *The Story Map* as my guide.

People say to join clubs or activities to meet new people and to say "hi" to maybe get a conversation going at some point.

Even though I didn't feel like it because the whole thing felt so weird, I got up the courage to start saying "hi."

I even joined a club I really like a lot now.

Over time, I made new friends, making the new school feel more like home.

I realized that change can be tough to get used to.

But if I hang in there and try new things, even if they feel weird, change can also lead to exciting experiences and new friendships!

Messed-Up Room Example

What's Happening

Imagine that your mom sat you down to discuss your messy room. You think that as long as you close the door why should anyone else care if there is a big mess in there? Your mom tries to explain that this responsibility is part of growing up. You don't agree. Your mom and you are both upset. And you don't know what to do.

The ATM Way: Acknowledge Your Emotions. Then Team Up with Your Brain (Breathe) To Make a Plan for Building Your Best Adventure with The Story Map as Your Guide.

What's Possible

I thought about compromising with my mom by setting a schedule for cleaning or finding a way to make cleaning my room more fun.

What's Next

I decided to talk to my mom and suggested that we could make a cleaning game out of it or set a specific day to clean together.

Happily Ever After

My mom liked the idea, and we turned cleaning into a fun activity. It still felt like a responsibility, but it became less of a hassle, and our relationship really improved.

Example of Writing Out a Messed-Up Room Story

My mom has been upset about my messy room for a while now, and finally said we have to sit down and talk about it.

I went first and told her I didn't see the problem if I kept the door closed so no one else had to look at it.

My mom said it bothers her even if she doesn't have to look right at it.

She thinks my keeping my room neater and cleaner is a responsible part of growing up that shows respect for others and myself too.

We both left our 'meeting' upset with no resolution, agreeing to try again another time.

Using *The ATM Way*, I stopped to notice what I was feeling in my body. Then I did my breaths to get my inside team up and ready to figure out how to deal with this using *The Story Map* as my guide.

I decided to ask her to help me at the beginning anyway because I felt pretty overwhelmed by the whole thing myself.

When I asked her if she could help me the first time, she said she loved the idea and thought it would be fun.

My mom and I are feeling good about each other. I am feeling good about myself. And I am loving living in my neater and cleaner space.

ABOUT THE AUTHOR

Madelaine Claire Weiss, LICSW, MBA, BCC, is a Harvard-trained Licensed Psychotherapist, Mindset Expert, and Board-Certified Executive, Career, and Life Coach. Madelaine created *Brainy* to help teach kids what her clients are learning that they wish they had learned much earlier in their lives.

She is the founder and former chair of The School-Business Partnership in Acton, Massachusetts, a Parenting Education Facilitator for the Massachusetts court system, and a current Outreach Volunteer with DC Tutoring and Mentoring Initiative (DCTMI) in Washington, DC.

Madelaine is a co-author in the *Handbook of Stressful Transitions Across the Lifespan* and bestselling author of *Getting to G.R.E.A.T.: 5-Step Strategy for Work and Life.*

She is a former administrative director of a group mental health practice, a corporate chief organizational development officer, and an associate director of an educational resource program at Harvard Medical School.

Madelaine has been featured on *NBC, W4WRadio, Fox TV*, and *Talk4TV*; has written for *Thrive Global* and *Authority Magazine's Editor's List*; is an opinion columnist for *CEOWorld Magazine*; and led webinars for *MedSense*, the *American Bar Association, Harvard Law School Association,* and the *International Association of Business Communicators.*

Madelaine has two grown, married children and five grandchildren, all of whom she adores.

A Special Note
from Madelaine

Dear Kids, may this book guide you on a fun and exciting path to learning and discovery.

Dear Parents and Teachers, may this book support you as you help your precious children to grow joyfully.

We're thrilled you've joined us on this journey. If you enjoyed the book, please consider leaving a review and telling a friend! And, for updates on new releases and special offers, contact me at **madelaineweiss.com**.

Thank You!

* 9 7 9 8 9 9 0 8 9 4 2 0 4 *